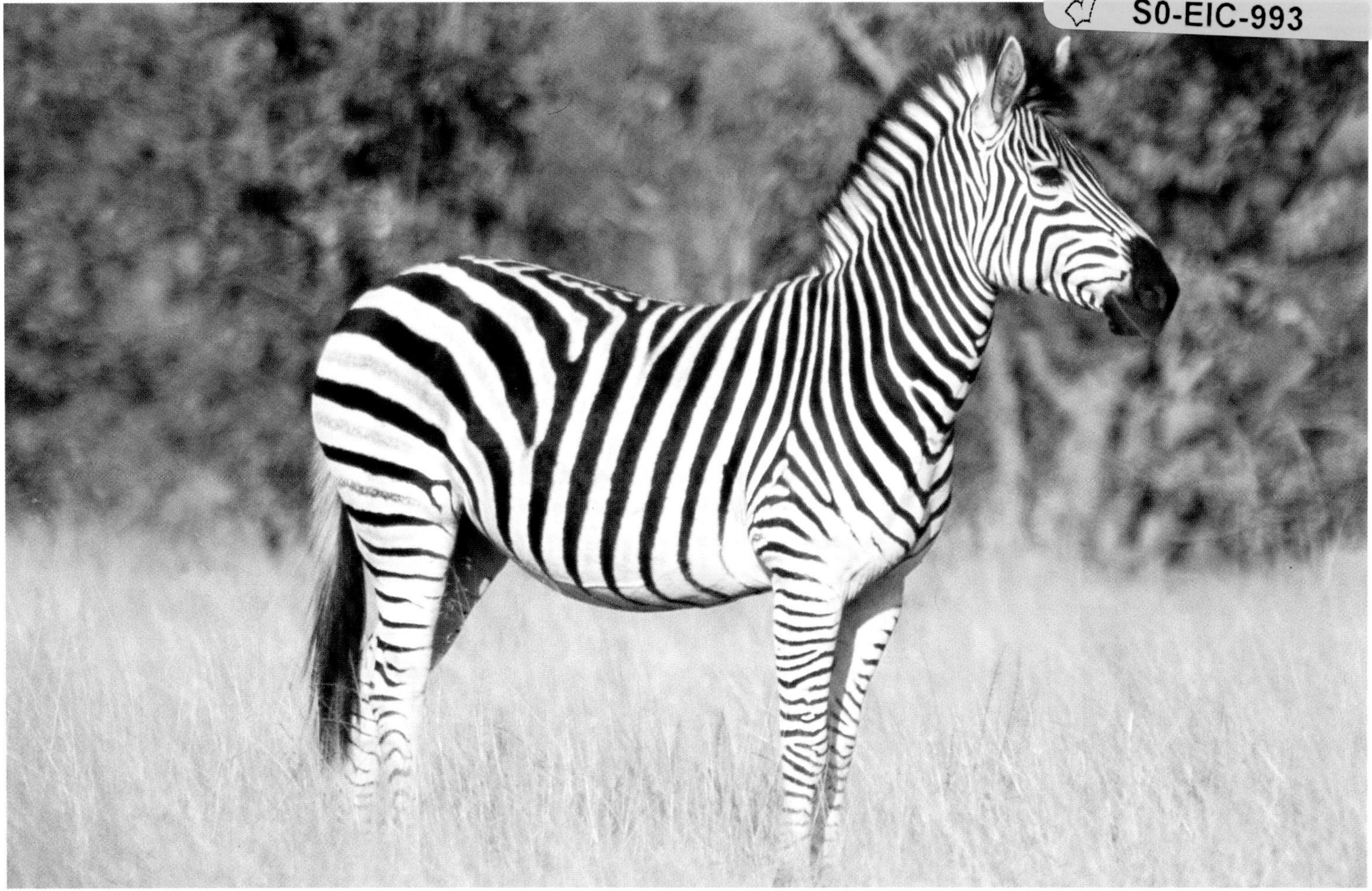

zebra

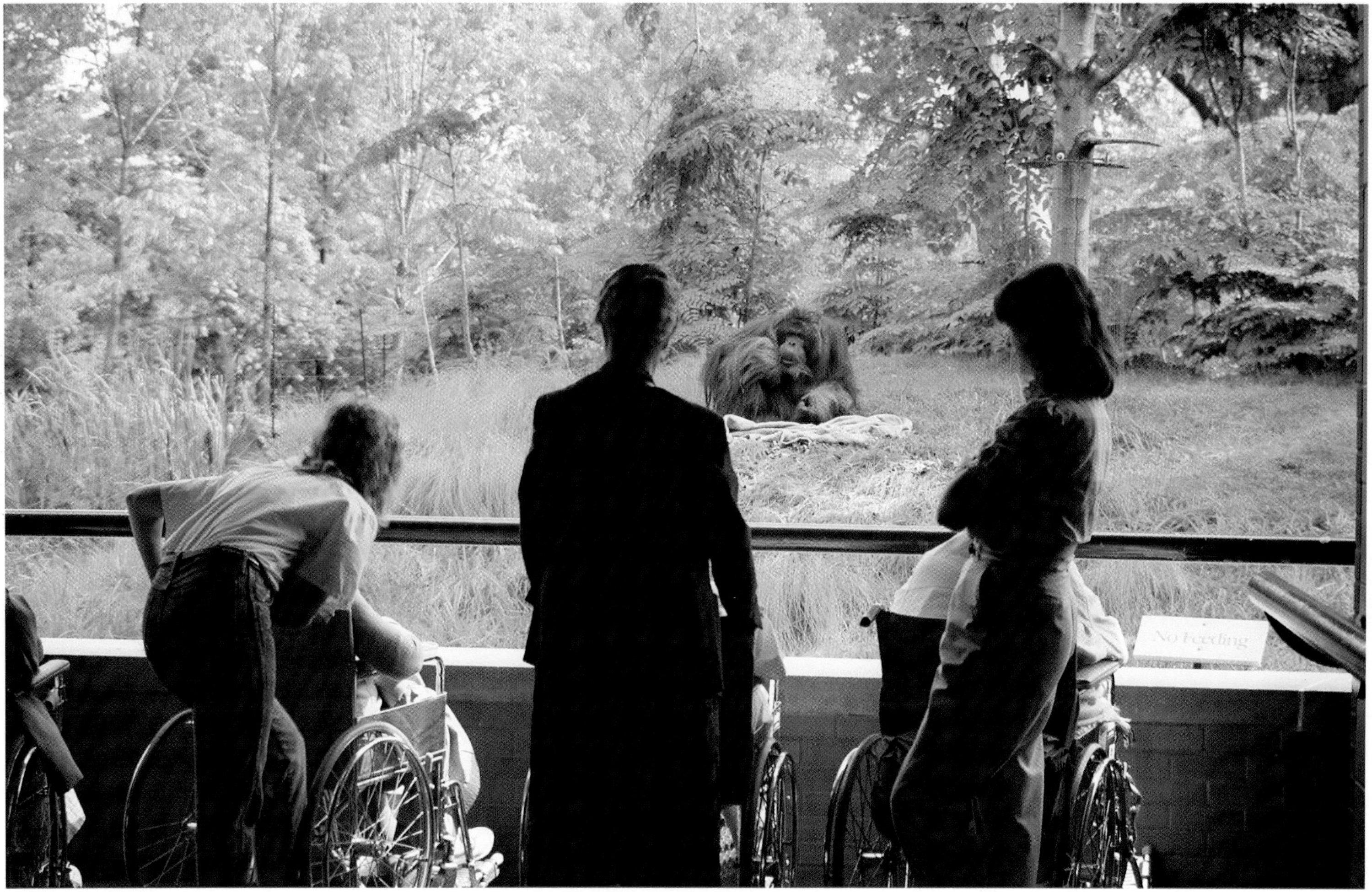

ZOO

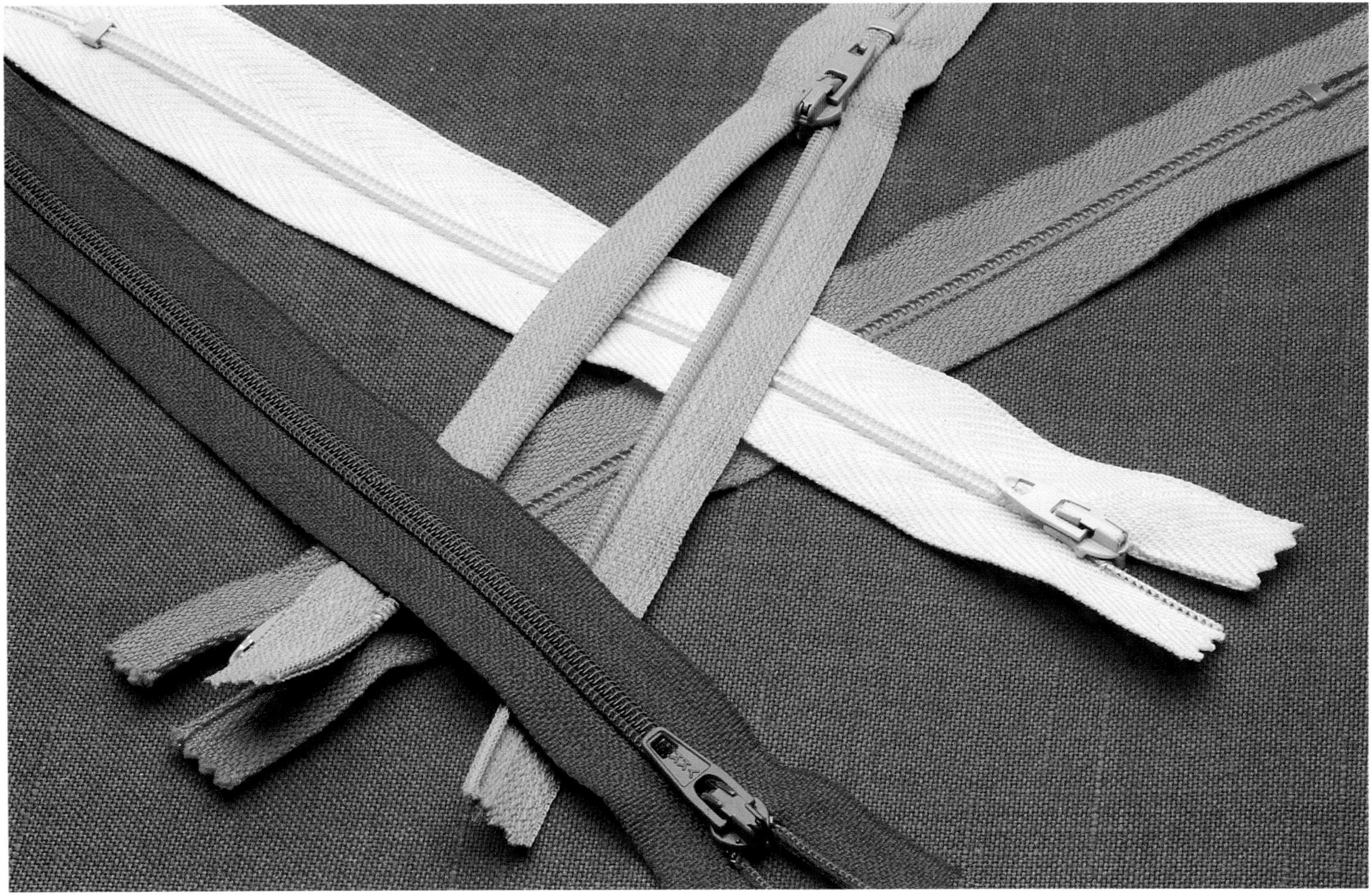

zippers

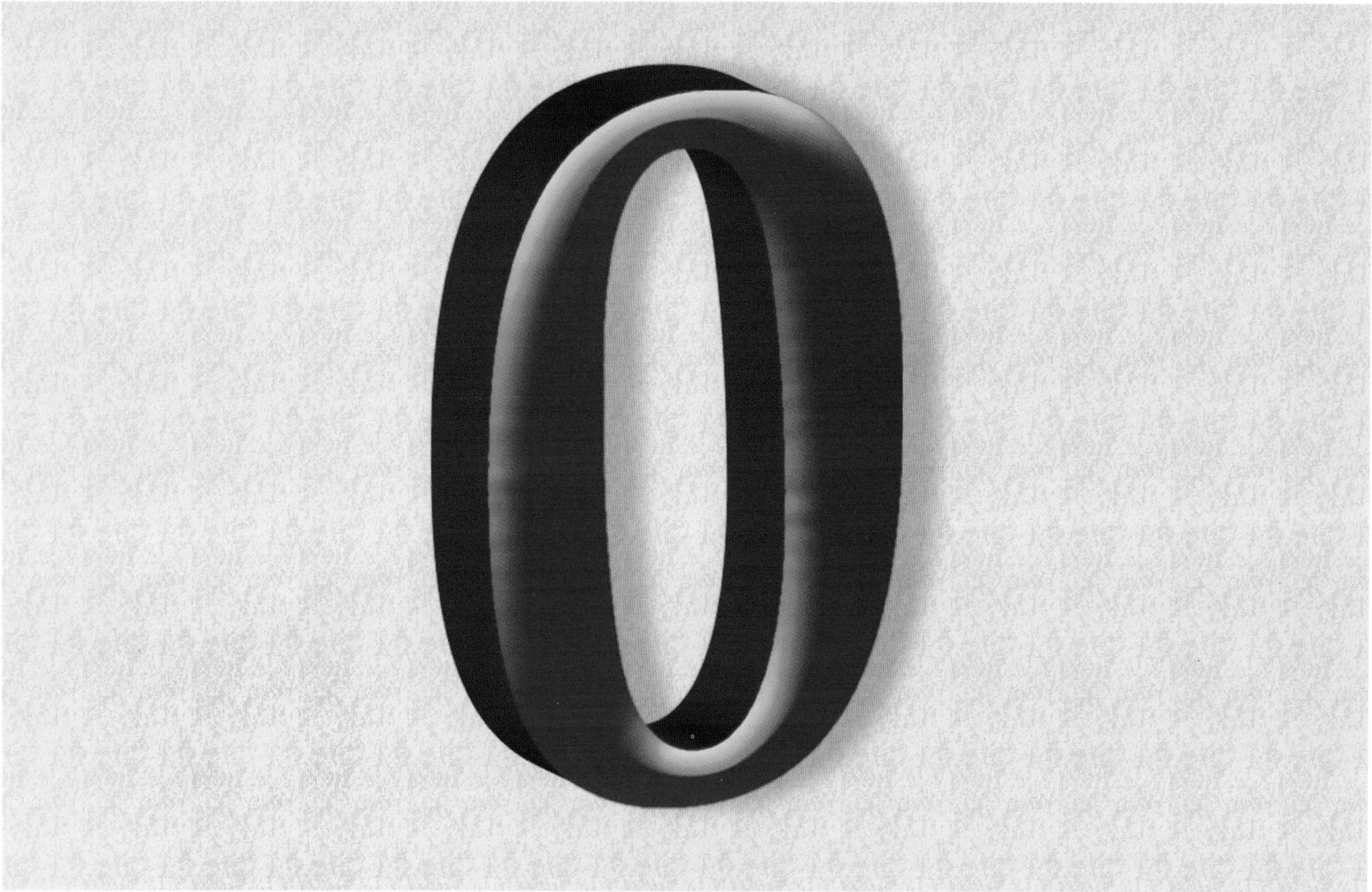

zero

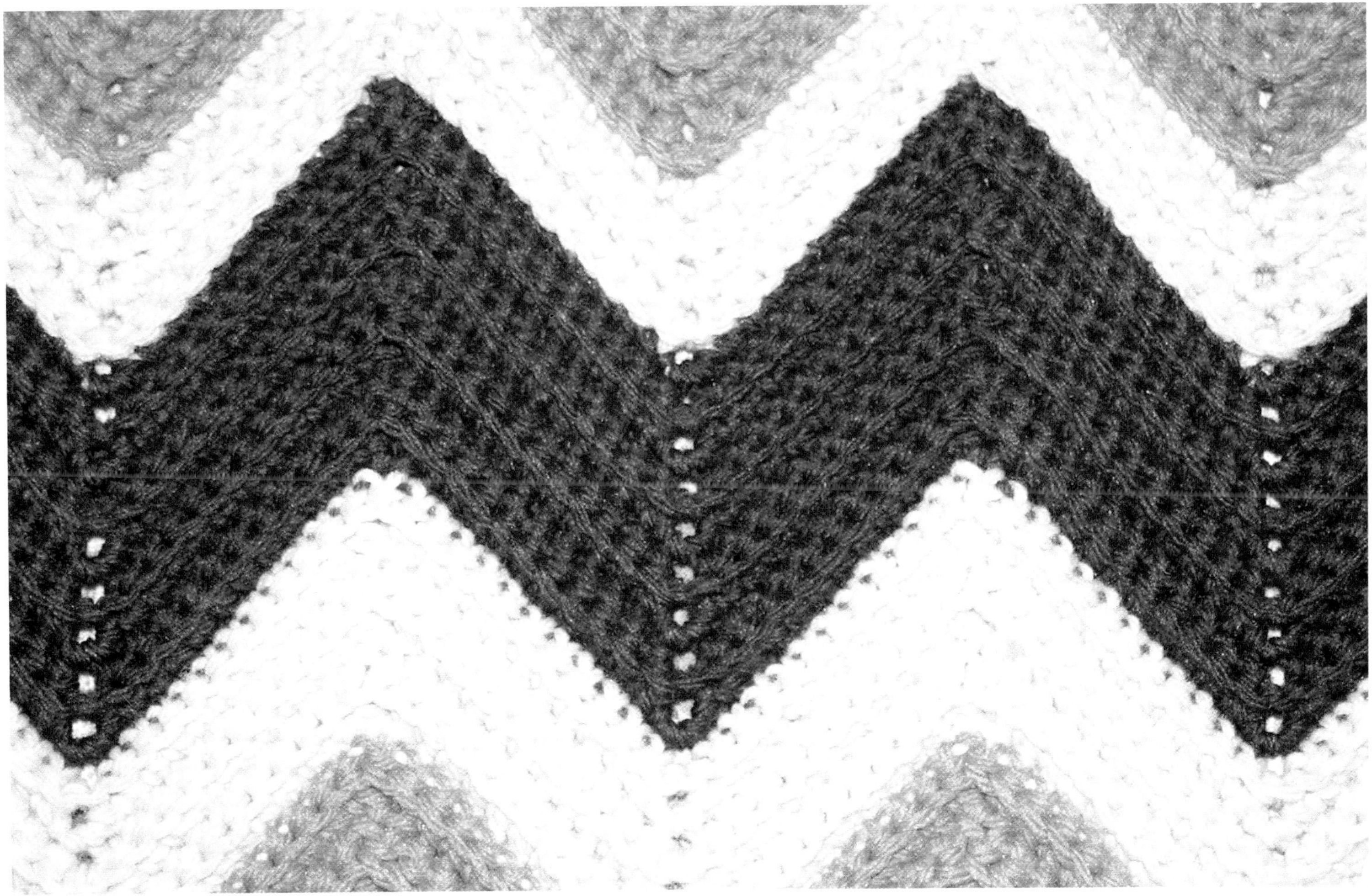

zigzag

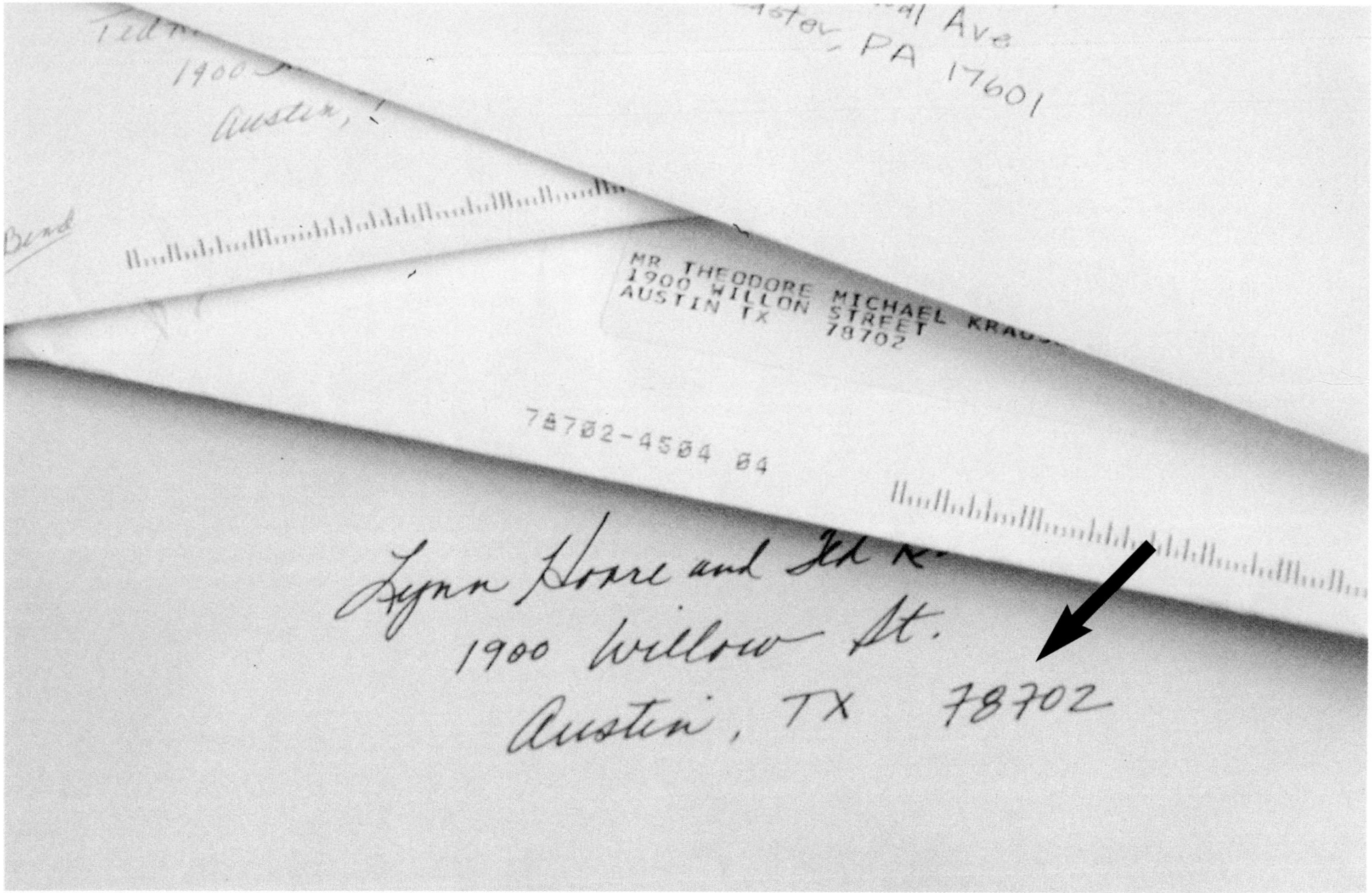
PA 17601
MR THEODORE MICHAEL
1900 WILLOW STREET
AUSTIN TX 78702
78702-4504 04
1900 Willow St.
Austin, TX 78702

zip code

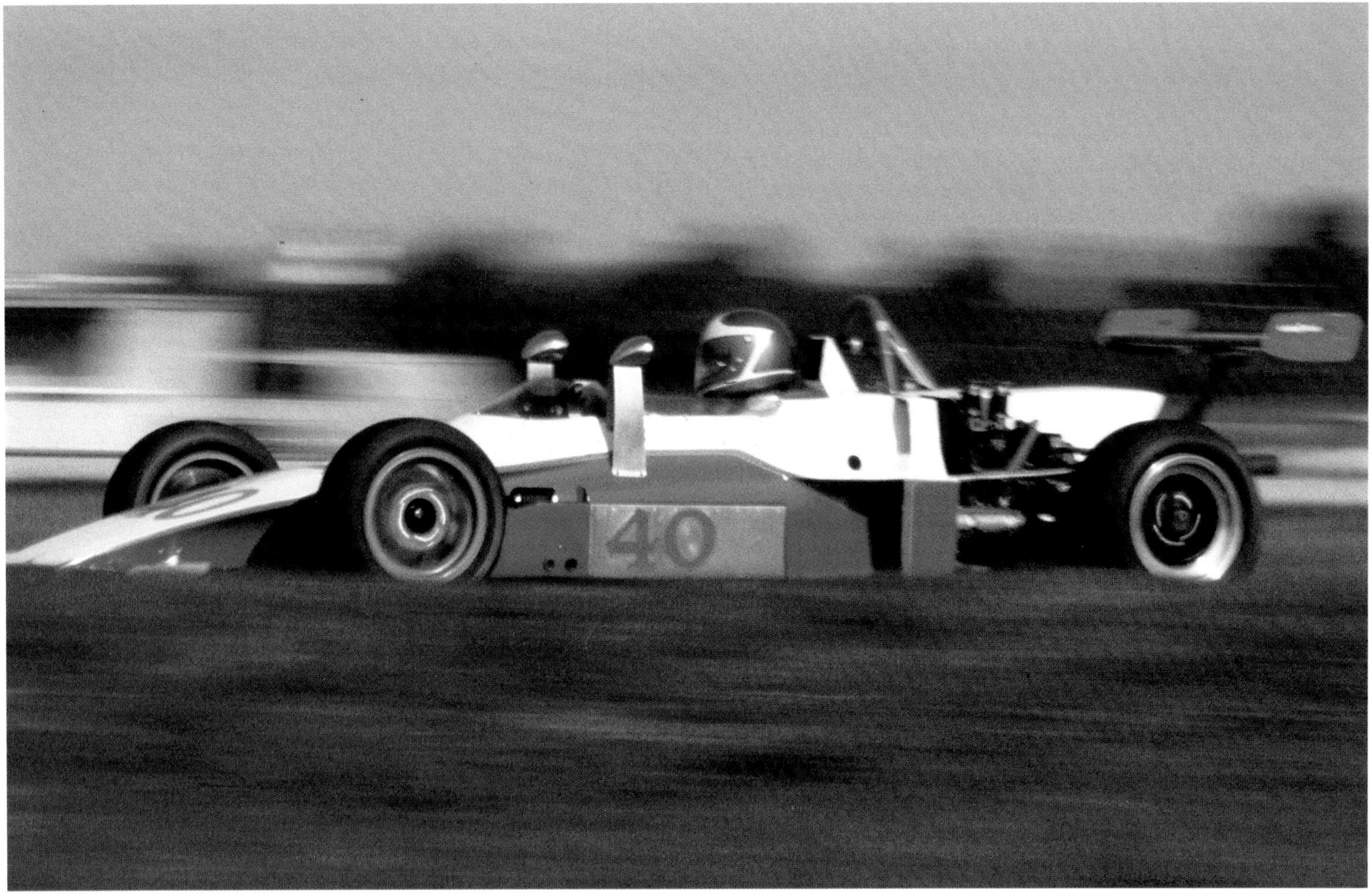

zoom

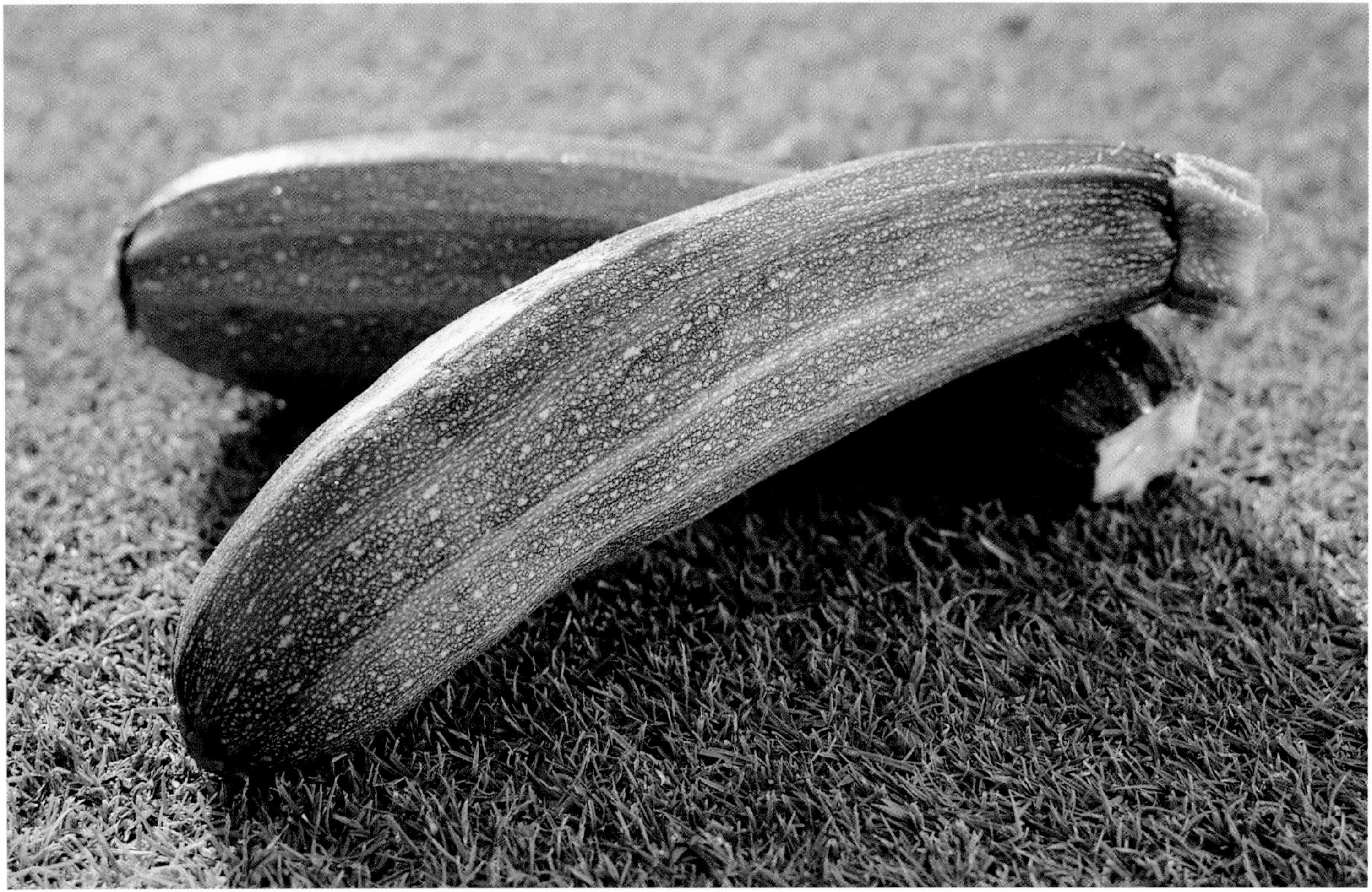

zucchini